NEBRASKA GOVERNOR RACE IN YEAR 2022

[Nebraska Governor Election results 2022]

Political news from
Nelma Tessa

Copyright©2022 Nelma Tessa 4

All Right Reserved 4

THE ELECTION RESULTS AND RACE
PREDICTIONS...5

Breakdown by the type of vote in Nebraska...6

Nebraska Republicans...............................7

HIS DEMOCRATIC OPPONENT 9

Pillen 10

A RE-NOMINATED, REPUBLICAN...............13

2022 Nebraska primaries 18

Governor 19

2022 Nebraska Governor's Race 19

RURAL COUNTIES ELECTION RESULTS...........27

THE ELECTION RESULTS AND RACE PREDICTIONS

The Associated Press provided election results and race predictions. Based on historical turnout figures and reporting from The Associated Press, The New York Times estimates the number of votes still to be cast. These are simply estimations, and official election reports may or may not corroborate them.

The results team of the New York Times is made up of graphic editors, engineers, and reporters that create and maintain software that allows the newspaper to publish election results in real time as they are provided by results providers.

Breakdown by the type of vote in Nebraska

Some states and counties give results broken down by the type of ballot cast, which can include votes cast on Election Day or early ballots cast in person or by mail. In Nebraska, that information isn't readily available.

The total number of votes expected in a contest after all votes are tabulated is known as the expected vote. This figure is an estimate based on numerous factors, including information on the number of votes cast early and information provided to our vote reporters by county election authorities on Election Day. As NBC News acquires fresh information, the figure may change.

Nebraska Republicans

Nebraska Republicans chose Jim Pillen as their gubernatorial nominee, choosing the University of Nebraska regent favored by the state's departing governor over a rival backed by former President Donald

The statewide loss in Nebraska on Tuesday was a setback for Trump. In a bid to sway the GOP in his favor ahead of a prospective presidential candidacy in 2024, he has issued hundreds of endorsements and held his typical campaign-style rallies in support of his chosen candidates, including Herbster.

Herbster's defeat elevates the stakes in other high-profile contests in Pennsylvania and Georgia this month, where Trump has also participated in campaigns.

HIS DEMOCRATIC OPPONENT

Pillen will be a favorite against his Democratic opponent, state Sen. Carol Blood, in November's general election in this Republican stronghold. Since 1994, Nebraska has not had a Democrat as governor.

Governor Pete Ricketts, former Governor Kay Orr, and famed former University of Nebraska football coach and congressman Tom Osborne were among those who endorsed Pillen. Term constraints precluded Ricketts from running again.

The charges against Herbster, a longstanding Trump supporter, didn't stop Trump from having a rally with him earlier this month in Nebraska.

Pillen

Lindstrom congratulated Pillen on his victory and said he would support him in the general election.

In a story last month, the Nebraska Examiner interviewed six women who claimed Herbster had groped their buttocks, outside of their clothes, during political events or beauty pageants. A seventh woman said Herbster once cornered her privately and kissed her forcibly.

One of the accusers, Republican state Sen. Julie Slama, said Herbster reached up her skirt and touched her inappropriately at the Douglas County Republican Party's annual Elephant Remembers dinner in 2019. The

Associated Press does not typically identify people who say they are victims of sexual assault unless they choose to come forward publicly, as Slama has done.

Herbster sued Slama for defamation, alleging that she falsely implicated him in an attempt to destroy his campaign. Slama filed a countersuit alleging sexual battery against Herbster.

Some people indicated the charges had no effect on their decision to vote for Herbster.

Joann Kotan said she was "upset by the stories, but I'm not sure if I believe them" as she voted at an elementary school in northwest Omaha on Tuesday. "I voted for Herbster because President Trump endorsed him," the 74-year-old remarked.

Lindstrom was also targeted, with Ricketts funding third-party television commercials portraying him as too liberal for the conservative state.

.

Lindstrom is shown standing in front of a rainbow flag with a coronavirus mask overlaid over his face in one digitally manipulated commercial.

Devon Leesley endorsed Lindstrom, 41, because "it's time to pass over the reins of politics to the next generation." Both Pillen and Herbster are in their sixties.

Leesley, a 45-year-old Omaha resident, said he didn't pay attention to the numerous endorsements in the contest.

A RE-NOMINATED, REPUBLICAN

Secretary of State Bob Evnen, a Republican who was also re-nominated on Tuesday, anticipated that 35% of registered voters will vote in the primary, the highest percentage since 2006, based on what he had seen so far.

Republican U.S. Rep. Jeff Fortenberry resigned from office and lost his reelection bid in March after being found guilty of federal corruption charges.

Mike Flood, a former speaker of the Nebraska Legislature, received the Republican candidacy, while Patty Pansing Brooks received the Democratic nomination. Flood is a solid favorite in the Republican-leaning 1st Congressional District, which encompasses Lincoln, small towns, and a big area of eastern Nebraska farmland.

Despite Trump's loss in the Nebraska governor's race, his influence was critical in West Virginia's primary elections, which were held on the same day. Rep. Alex Mooney, Trump's candidate, defeated Rep. David McKinley in a race pitting two Republican incumbents against each other. McKinley had angered Trump by voting for President Joe Biden's bipartisan infrastructure package and the establishment of the House committee investigating the Jan. 6 attack on the US Capitol.

Herbster, who chaired former President Donald Trump's (R) Agriculture and Rural Advisory Committee, described himself as a "political outsider, businessman, and fifth-generation farmer and rancher" who believes it is "time for a Nebraska farmer and rancher to lead our great state toward successful solutions." [6] [7] "America is in trouble, and if

America is in trouble, Nebraska is in trouble," Herbster said. "Governors will have two duties moving forward: to lead their states and to push back against government overreach that's flowing out of Washington like a tsunami." [8] In October 2021, Trump endorsed Herbster. [9] Herbster was endorsed by Nebraska Lt. Gov. Mike Foley (R) in March 2022. [10].

Lindstrom is a senator in Nebraska's state legislature. He claimed to have "been at the vanguard of tax reform, economic development, and family concerns," as well as having "authored legislation to make college more affordable for Nebraskans, defended the unborn, and led the battle against the opioid crisis." [11] Lindstrom "indicated" that he "had the potential to connect with the next generation of leadership while also bringing substantial legislative expertise to the governor's office," according to Walton. [12] Lindstrom was backed by Omaha Mayor Jean Stothert and the Nebraska State Education Association in April 2022. [13] [14]

Pillen, a veterinarian and owner of Pillen Family Farms, is a University of Nebraska Regent "I will seek to expand our economy and provide every youngster in Nebraska with the opportunity to follow their ambitions. Our flawed property tax system must be fixed, and taxes must be reduced. We need to reform our tax code, extend broadband access, and upgrade infrastructure throughout the state." [15] In January 2022, Ricketts endorsed Pillen, and the Nebraska Farm Bureau endorsed him in February. [16] [17]

Aaron Sanderford of the Nebraska Examiner reported on April 14, 2022, that eight women have accused Herbster of sexual assault between 2017 and 2022.

[18]

Herbster refuted the charges.

Donna was also running in the primary. Michael Connely, Lela McNinch, Breland Ridenour, Theresa Thibodeau, and Troy Wentz are among the cast members. The deadline for submissions was March 1, 2022. [20]

Major independent observers classified the general election as Solid/Safe Republican as of May 2022. Rickets was first elected in 2014 and re-elected in 2018, defeating state Senator Bob Krist (D) by a margin of 59-41. Since 1999, Republicans have controlled all three branches of state government in Nebraska.

2022 Nebraska primaries

Nebraska's governor's race is the most contested election in the state this year. Gov. Pete Ricketts (R) is term-limited and both parties are hosting contested primaries. The winner of the Republican primary is likely to be favored in November – President Donald Trump won Nebraska by 19 points in 2020.

Governor

The Republican primary will be another test of Trump's influence in Nebraska. Trump-endorsed businessman Charles Herbster, who has been accused by multiple women of sexual assault, faces a long list of challengers, including University of Nebraska's Board of Regents member Jim Pillen, who was endorsed by Ricketts. On the Democratic side, state Sen. Carol Blood has just one challenger, Roy Harris.

2022 Nebraska Governor's Race

Republican voters Tuesday awarded the lead to University of Nebraska Regent and Columbus hog producer Jim Pillen in the hard-fought contest to replace Nebraska Governor Pete Ricketts.

Ricketts and other powerful Nebraska Republicans backed Pillen in a bitter primary that roiled the Republican electorate, and the results were a win for them. Former President Donald Trump endorsed Pillen's closest rival, Charles W. Herbster, during a visit to the state in the run-up to a three-way election.

Pillen had an approximately 7,000 vote advantage over Herbster, a Falls City cattle rancher and Republican mega-donor who runs various enterprises, according to election authorities. Senator Brett Lindstrom, who had surged to the top of the polls early Tuesday, has dropped to third place.

Late Tuesday night, both Herbster and Lindstrom conceded.

The enthusiasm in the Embassy Suites in Lincoln, where Pillen and his family had gathered with over 100 supporters, grew as the night went. Ricketts, whose term is coming to an end, spoke to the gathering early in the evening.

Pillen has highlighted his tough opinions on hot-button national issues including abortion and critical race theory since almost the beginning of his candidacy.

His campaign was stacked with seasoned Nebraska political operators, including some Ricketts campaign veterans. Former Governor Kay Orr, former U.S. Representative and Husker football coach Tom Osborne, and the Nebraska Farm Bureau were among his backers.

The Nebraska Farm Bureau's Mark McHargue praised Pillen's grassroots efforts while campaigning across the state. Pillen, who notably did not participate in any of the pre-election debates, embarked on a six-stop tour of the state with a few of his most powerful supporters just a day before the election.

However, not all Nebraska Republicans backed him.

As Pillen and Herbster attempted to outflank each other from the right, the race became increasingly heated. The schism became clear in October, when Trump revealed his support for Herbster, prompting Ricketts to declare Herbster unfit for the job.

Multiple polls indicated that the race was a three-way race between Pillen, Herbster, and Lindstrom as election day approached. Herbster and Lindstrom were the focus of the first wave of third-party attack ads, which began airing in March.

Negative advertising invaded the contest at a volume that analysts thought was unparalleled in modern times, eventually targeting all three contenders.

Ricketts contributed over $1.3 million to Conservative Nebraska, a political action committee, in March and April. The ads initially targeted Herbster, but later moved their focus to Lindstrom, claiming that he was not a true conservative. It released two fresh anti-herbster campaign a week before the election.

Herbster's candidacy was defined in many respects by his resemblance to and endorsement from Trump, who visited Nebraska for a rally in Greenwood on May 1. Herbster also had the support of South Dakota Governor Kristi Noem, former United States Representative Lee Terry, and former Omaha Mayor and United States Representative Hal Daub.

The contest was thrown into disarray in mid-April when the Nebraska Examiner published allegations from eight women alleging Herbster had touched them at events in prior years.

Powerful Nebraska lawmakers were quick to condemn the incident, but not unanimously.

Herbster flatly disputed the claims, claiming they were staged by Ricketts and Pillen as a political hit job. Herbster has filed a defamation suit against a Republican state legislator who is one of the accusers.

Herbster appeared to concede the contest shortly after 11 p.m. Tuesday, saying he had called Pillen to congratulate him. Herbster said he will continue to battle to eliminate critical race theory and sex education from

Nebraska schools while thanking his campaign team and supporters.

Herbster called the governor election one of the "nastiest" in Nebraska history, and those in the audience agreed, adding "in the country." Herbster expressed disappointment that the negative publicity had an impact on the outcomes, although not mentioning the claims against him.

"We didn't lose," declared Jack Brewer, a former NFL player and prominent Trump supporter, soon before Herbster was introduced. "Today, Nebraska lost."

Herbster's supporter, State Senator Tom Briese, stated Pillen will have his "full support" moving forward. Despite the fact that the race was "extremely acrimonious," Briese believes it is critical for Republicans to "convalesce" around the winner and promote conservative ideas in November's general election against Democratic nominee Sen. Carol Blood of Bellevue.

Lindstrom also stated that he will be sponsoring Pillen, whom he congratulated. The two-term lawmaker acknowledged his supporters and family members at a watch party in Omaha Tuesday night.

"It's just part of politics sometimes," Lindstrom remarked when asked how he came to thank Pillen after his supporters insulted him during the election.

RURAL COUNTIES ELECTION RESULTS

While some rural counties were yet to post results as of late Tuesday, Pillen was outpolling Herbster outside of Nebraska's three largest counties.

Lindstrom won by a large margin in Douglas County, but Pillen and Herbster were neck and neck.

Pillen was outperforming Herbster in Lancaster County.

Herbster showed strong in Sarpy County, where he was nearly even with Lindstrom and defeated Pillen by over 1,000 votes just after midnight. However, it did not appear to be enough to overcome Pillen's statewide relative strength.

Pillen addressed his supporters, expressing his "passion for Nebraska" and promising to work to improve the state for future generations.

He stated, "We're going to focus on what's best for Nebraska."